Down by the creek, near the Cottonwoods

Lauren Wolf

BookLeaf Publishing

India | USA | UK

Down by the creek, near the Cottonwoods ©
2024 Lauren Wolf

Presentation by *BookLeaf Publishing*

Web: www.bookleafpub.com

E-mail: info@bookleafpub.com

ISBN: 9789358318166

First edition 2024

DEDICATION

To Mika Chan, quién me acompañó hasta el final, con dulzura y amor infiníto.

PREFACE

Once upon a time in ancient lands, a girl was born who filled her summers coloring in notebooks with portraits of bird goddesses, collecting nature samples and gluing them in her journals, writing poems and studying people. She continued this as she grew, losing it from time to time. Every time she recovered her practices, she realized that she was letting her true soul shine and grow. Here are the words of winter 2023 that spring out of her, and into this tumultuous world.

My true gnome

Wondering what you eat for
breakfast
Wondering what humans and situations
hold your attention in awe
Wondering how I got it,
then lost it, so quickly.
As I look at the sky, sunset, and wind rustle
the leaves with grace and poise,
so do I avoid thinking of your dark,
fickle gaze.
1,000 times preferable is the silent gaze
and continuous smile of the garden gnome:
always content to be nestled
in the damp leaves of my garden-
always present, no matter the weather.

Alive

Feeling the breeze in my hair
and the hot stone beneath my bum,
I watch the turquoise water flow around me.
It is cool and refreshing.
I sip on the passion fruit juice,
and listen to the children's laughter and shrieks
as they swim by.
I think of the thousands that are sitting at their
desks, ageing slowly under fluorescent lights,
and a hundred times over
I choose this trip, this flight, this solo
wandering beyond borders,
and will continue to choose to push myself
beyond borders,
as long as I'm alive!

24 K

Today as I looked at the paintings
with gold leaf,
I wondered what I would feel confident enough
to emboss with gold?
I think about your salty kiss and smile
as your hands wrapped around me
and lifted me up through the ocean waves,
or the clink of the ice
in the cup as we put our feet in the river,
the tent and campfire at our backs.
I think about the time
your car spun backwards, through the traffic
light, downhill, through a snowstorm,
to get to me on my birthday.
I think about the time
we made love under the stars in the mountain
and it was freezing cold.
I think about dancing pegadito,
and while I may not put gold leaf around
anything I paint, all of these memories with you
are 24 K, my love.

Only in my dreams

Do you move your finger like a paintbrush
in circles around my belly button before
you kiss me,
Do I wait for you
with only the candle lit,
naked and half-asleep,
do we skinny dip in the lake under the full
moon,
and hold hands as we gaze across
the city lights from high above,
do we share a warm piece of fresh bread from
the panadería, and you compare it to my ass,
do I twirl your curly hair between my fingers
as I fall asleep.

Winter Wonderland

It's snowing outside
and I can see the smoke rise from my breath
As I rush to shut the door.
I have heard of people who take ice baths
or ski naked
and here I am,
content to remain fully snuggled,
thousands of miles away, my feet nestled in the
blanket, a fireplace ablaze,
dreaming of hearing the train whistle outside,
and having a cup of hot chocolate with you.

CrossFit

Feeling my hands rougher,
more calloused,
thinking of the weights to pull,
and boxes to jump on. It's much more preferable
to hear my lungs
gasp and find it hard to breath,
than to bear the unbearable sadness of
this world's wars and abandoned humans.
Hanging from the bar is a sure way
to be in the present moment
and leave the day behind.
As I wash away the sweat,
my muscles sleep content, knowing that by
pushing them, I gain a little peace:
reconnecting
body, spirit, breath, and mind.

Perfect alignment

Tonight as I drove home
I saw a perfect alignment of about 13 stars
in a 45 degree straight line stretching
up from the horizon,
full moon on the horizon,
Perfect alignment for a hug from the kids,
Perfect alignment for all prisoners to be
released,
Perfect alignment for a gifted cup of coffee,
Perfect alignment for a small dance,
Perfect alignment for sitting with the silence of a
no-response,
Perfect alignment for the wind to whistle,
Perfect alignment for humans to not yet pass
environmental-protective laws, but want to,
Perfect alignment for a little kiss on my belly
rolls,
Perfect alignment for sharing an extra apple in
my car with an unhoused human,
Perfect alignment to light a candle,
Perfect alignment to open a new book and hug
my brain,
Perfect alignment for me to give thanks
for another day
in this beautiful life!

Your sweet face and paws

Your tiny nose and nails
that just know the state of the world,
with their proximity.
For weeks, months, and years,
you have grown with and near me.
They say goodbye is an illusion, like time,
and I know that I've whispered to you
how I will carry my love for you forever
with each of my words, actions, and steps.
Yet it doesn't make it any easier.
Connecting with you in peace, love,
curiosity, and for all the emotions,
gives meaning to this pale blue dot.
So, I kiss your sweet face and paws,
one more time; thank you.
Now you are free to go throw up and pee in
someone else's houseplants and shoes,
to roll in too much catnip and eat too many
cookies after you have looked at me with your
sad forsaken eyes to which I always gave in;
enjoy little master!

The trail

I thought I heard a beautiful, deep voice, offer
solace in the warmth depths of the mountain,
after we quarreled and I ran from you across the
field.
His voice is beautiful, and his eyes are
enchanting, and the language is full of twists and
turns and scents so different from our realm.
While our embrace feels eternal, I am mostly
alone.
Days pass into months,
and my memories blur, mixing together this
intoxicating, dark hibernation,
both cold, and firey, and full of stones,
with natural and comforting warmth and buzzing
crickets,
prickly grass and blooming flowers
of our days in the sun and fields.
Oh mother, Demeter, there they are!
Your wonderfully red, juicy seeds,
creating the brightest trail;
the beating life-force you have promised me! As
I lean over to pick up each one
and savor it's explosive juice in my mouth, the
light grows brighter,
I begin to see the river,

my mind becomes clearer,
I can breathe easier...
each step walking closer to you,
to my home, and to our beautiful Spring
and Summer.

Los sistemas of Satyagraha

Systems.. ever changing.
The only constant is change.
"They" to speak about 1 human,
"Elle" en vez de él o ella,
The systems of power and light,
darkness and fragility,
cultures are formed, molded, and destroyed,
deconstructed, or upheld daily.
Mi único deseo, my one wish,
as I age, may be to maintain curiosity over
certainty.
If certainty can be so fixed
as to throw hate and fear like confetti,
rather than hold each other up,
then I never want it.
In whatever language you engage,
to build and share,
crear y preguntar,
only the unknown is where we find wonder,
love, and peace.
We must venture into the darkness of these
systems, estos sistemas, with an artist's
mind of creativity and wonder.
Inventar,
Romper,

Desconstruir...

Invent
Break
Deconstruct...

Only then can one be limitless, ageless,
and find, share, and spread true
Satyagraha

Radical acceptance

Radical acceptance of your divine thighs
having grown in depth proportions to the
exquisitely beautiful red wood tree rings.
Radical acceptance of how the sweet curve
of your cheek
reminds me of a perfect, smooth, peach colored
shoreline, whose waves roll in
with laughter.
Radical acceptance that human population is
both exploding and waning as I sit next to you
enraptured.
Radical acceptance of unexpected goodbyes,
replaced by the sweet sound of the quiet air
whispering 'what is next'?
Radical acceptance of salty tears
behind the child's fear or confusion.
Radical acceptance of random laughter
throughout kitchens as neighbors cook and
nourish.
Radical acceptance of the cold fog that
brings my auntie, and hundreds of other bundled
hearts, a bit of arthritis aches,
a reminder of this ephemeral life, making their
bones yell 'I'm still here!

That fall you had wasn't great 30 years ago, but
here we are!!!"
Radical acceptance of the thousands of tent
homes for unhoused people, for the social
inequity of earned income as trash dumps
continue to fill higher and higher, consumerism
still being wildly popular.
Radical acceptance for the wind whistling
around the Cottonwood leaves,
as the prairie dogs pop up from their holes in
quiet observance, while others chirp the
warnings and news...

of now and what's to come.

Being comfortable

A compliment I recently received
Was how they admire how comfortable I am
In my own skin.
As with many compliments,
I blushed as I took in their love.
As with many compliments,
My brain began to psycho -analyze, and dissect
them..
"If you only knew how often I am not",
I thought.
Luckily, my spirit stopped my fear and heard
their words behind the words, heard their
longing and admiration intertwined, heard their
recognition of what I think they're already really
good at, and their disconnect from their own
comfort;
and my heart grew bigger to hold us both
together in my skin
at that moment.
What we see when we look at others
is truly what we see in ourselves.

Comfortable? I am a privileged human, who is
in a position in life where I can express myself
authentically; this I am.

However, I constantly reflect, edit, shift,
as I try to adapt this wild self
to the environment and people around me.

Pain? It's a constant, and I nurture it with
Hope.
Wounds that still unconsciously guide me?
I must develop practices to heal them and
let them rest, rather than lead,
and I often fail.

My own skin is something so flexible that I both
admire and pick at.
Comfort in it?
Thank you;
I am working on it!

Space for possibility

I heard that a famous guru says
30 min of meditation in am and pm will give
you...
Space for possibility!

What is your space like? Is it big, soft, hard,
easy to find, tasty, wet, cold, dry, noisy, quiet?

Let's go!

Do you want to come to mine? Mine is fucking
gorgeous, even with random sprinkles of pain;
that what makes the glittery parts sparkle even
brighter.

Do you share yours with others? How often do
you visit it? What emotion do you most feel in
it?

What if these spaces were for everyone and not
'exclusive'; I mean,
free, in public, and part of culture?
Gasp.. possibility?

Possibility for truly agnostic minds, from the
original definition of agnostic, of dark
knowledge, for wonderfully present blank
minds, for still minds, for free minds to share
and repopulate?

That may be too politically dangerous...
Dreaming and sharing and laughing and loving
without abandon, altogether??

All ages, shapes, sexes, genders, sizes,
languages, inhaling and exhaling past, present,
and future, in combined dharmas, karma,
swirling Samsara?

Possibility ...

10 days!

10 days until I jump into your arms,
10 days until I step into your air and
droplets of sweat begin to glisten down my skin
as your humidity envelops me,
10 days until I run shrieking into your waves and
taste the drops of salty water on my lips and
body, the sun baking everything
into a dreamy mirage,
10 days until I dig my toes and hands 4 inches
into you to feel a cool softness
 wrap around my fingers,
10 days until I toss back shots of mezcal
with an orange slice in your busy streets of
warm bodies, short dresses
swaying down the malecón,
10 days until you pull me on
your dance floors and my hips groove and grind
this year behind,
10 days until I get to hug you and smell you,
México querido, cómo te amo!!!
Allá te caigo, allá voy!!

Down by the creek, near the Cottonwoods

is where you'll find me
in peace.

In any time of reflection, introspection, or just
needing to connect,
if you walk down by the creek,
near the Cottonwoods,
that's where you'll find me,
bending over to pick up twigs
and see if I can break them
right on their knuckle,
to release the tiny star within,
like the old legend says.

Thanks to you,
I now better understand how to
listen to the wind,
as I would listen to a wise elder's song.
Thanks to you
I can feel brave enough to ask for help,
not just from my breath in yoga,
but from my fellow humyn.

During these winter days,

holidays and celebrations,
I observe the shifting tides in the rivers and
creeks.
As I slip my hands into the water and hold it as a
reflection,
I am reminded of the simple joy and beauty that
a noble friend, human,
Cottonwood, or waves,
can inspire.
As I see my soul flicker in the reflection,
if only for a second,
it is a reminder that the true decoration lights are
around us all year,
and shine in each smile, hug, and action.

Thank you for continuing to inspire me,
for continuing to dance with me
in this life.
I'll see you soon, down by the creek,
near the Cottonwoods...

Drishti

In the moment I read your message,
my drishti, my single focus,
being on your words and voice,
my heart felt as if it would explode!
Beating so fast, I felt as if I could fly over
the ocean to get to you,
to ride a train, or bike, or boat,
just to see your smile and the flash
of light across your
gorgeous eyes.
Now my drishti focuses on not just surviving,
but thriving a new season,
still without you,
still across the ocean,
and (re)creating that amazing,
intense heartbeat, that flushes through
my body with a lightning speed and heat,
with my art, writing,
and in my classroom and studies.
The drishti is always there,
eagle eyes with the long vantage point
in sight,
waiting patiently for the precise moment
to fly, and dive.

My Luck

I am lucky that I chose to be born
to these parents, in this family,
who are proud to have raised me
strong enough, and wild enough, to remind me
constantly of when I was 7 and declared,

"If any guy told me to cut my long hair off,
I would just say bye",

Driving and carrying me on their hips
where they could,
and then unleashing me to play outside, giving
plant and prairie tours which were only 2nd best
to books and art.

I am so very lucky, privileged, and blessed,
to be family with them,

so that after the rape,
I could still always seek refuge,
although my ability to trust was forever altered,

so that after domestic abuse,
I could have the strength to first go home,
regather the pieces of my soul,

and then continue on in my path for healing,
in my own way, with their support, and with
such a resolve and determination
which undoubtedly these deep roots helped to
nourish in the dead of winters.

My luck is that with the gift of time and
perspective, (with age), I am now able to see
how the seeds of
confidence, faith, beauty, joy, practicality,
and the ability to love with my heart wide open,
in the middle of hospital halls
during my brother's surgeries, in the middle of
pain and doubt,
(which they continued to water),

would ultimately grow be such thick jungle
vines to cling to in darkness, and which would
inevitably save me from mud and insanity,
clinging to them until the hurricane winds pass,
and I was again able to stand.

My luck is that 40 years later, I can realize and
celebrate with eyes wide open,
how I am but one of millions who glitter like
diamonds,
broken pieces of beautiful earth and sand, living
collections of particles, memories, and stardust,
all shimmering in the sunlight

as the tides rush in to wash and carry us out,
to begin anew.

Pandora's Box: Evolution and Growth

Year 2035:

AI bot #452673 stops in it's tracks through the snowstorm at night in the mountains, the blue moonlight making a beautiful glow. It turns to AI bot #317692 and asks,
"How did the humans ever expect to feel the joy without the pain?
Are they so different than the squirrels enjoying their Spring and Summertime food surplus while knowing they must continue to store in order to survive the snow?"

AI Bot #317692 responds, "for the last few thousands of years, in the winters, they mostly just focused on survival, and most recently they fall into a deep longing for certain traditions, places, and people
from their past,
until finally AI bot Pandora reopened her box in 2024.

When she did, the humans' brains and body cells were instantly flooded with the message

'let go of regret and longing; focus on creating
and celebrating current traditions, people and
places where you are, with beauty and love'...
'We all share pain, which spreads throughout our
hips brain, and heart.
Compassion, empathy and sharing
is most crucial!'.

"With these messages, combined with climate
change and one ecological disaster after another,
they began to unite with their similarities rather
than fear and separation. However, we still
cannot gauge if it is enough for them to save
themselves."

AI bot 452673 responds,
"ohhhh.. well, when it's so cold that just going
outside here in the woods freezes
my antennae, I question how this human
dilemma will continue to unfold:
Will they continue to shift and prioritize people
over profits?
Will they value resources as equal rights for all
to share, or still understand them as strategic
pieces to be conquered?"

"They have seemingly come so far, yet the
disasters they have created and need to clean up
often seem insurmountable."

As they continue on to heave the ancient box
through the snow, they begin their chant for
evolution:

"Basic needs of evolution:
Nutrients and movement!
(Harvest, dance, walk, run,
crouch, reach, collect),
Basic needs of evolution
begins with Circulation!
(Air and water through systems,
thoughts, ideas, (re)usage of materials)"

They stop to open the box and there in the
corner is the small spider, AI bot Pandora,
releasing yet another beautiful silk ribbon of
hope, flying high past the city and moving out to
sea.

And so she continues to spin, weave, and release
her ribbons of hope,
as all the AI bots watch humans attentively, as
weather forecasters do the winds,
keen to be ready for their final demise, or the
true Renaissance of evolution.